Maery
zari

5-MINUTE
BRAIN GAMES
for
CleVer
Kids

Puzzles and solutions
by Dr Gareth Moore
B.Sc (Hons) M.Phil Ph.D

Illustrations and cover
artwork by Chris Dickason

Designed by Tall Tree Ltd

5-MINUTE BRAIN GAMES for Clever Kids

Buster Books

First published in Great Britain in 2021 by Buster Books,
an imprint of Michael O'Mara Books Limited,
9 Lion Yard, Tremadoc Road, London SW4 7NQ

W www.mombooks.com/buster
f Buster Books
🐦 @BusterBooks
📷 @buster_books

Clever Kids is a trade mark of Michael O'Mara Books Limited.

Puzzles and solutions © Gareth Moore 2021

Illustrations and layouts © Buster Books 2021

A CIP catalogue record for this book is available from the British Library.

ISBN: 978-1-78055-740-3

2 4 6 8 10 9 7 5 3 1

Papers used by Buster Books are natural, recyclable products made of wood from
well-managed, FSC®-certified forests and other controlled sources. The manufacturing
processes conform to the environmental regulations of the country of origin.

Printed and bound in June 2021 by CPI Group (UK) Ltd,
108 Beddington Lane, Croydon, CR0 4YY, United Kingdom

MIX
Paper from
responsible sources
FSC® C020471

INTRODUCTION

Get ready to push your brain to the limit and challenge your intellect with these fun-filled games!

In this book, you'll find a wide range of puzzles, mind-benders and leaps of logic, including wordsearches, odd ones out, spot the differences and crosswords. There are over 100 activities for you to complete in any order you like.

Start each puzzle by reading the instructions. Sometimes this is the hardest part, so don't worry if you have to read them a few times to understand what they mean.

Once you're clear on what to do, it's time to battle your way to the answer. Can you complete each puzzle in five minutes or less? Time yourself and write down how long each game takes you in the space provided.

For an extra challenge, you can come back to each puzzle at a later date and see if you can complete it even faster.

If you really struggle with a puzzle, take a look at the answers at the back to see how it works, then try it again later and see if you can work it out the second time round.

Good luck, and have fun!

Introducing the Brain Games Master:
Gareth Moore, B.Sc (Hons) M.Phil Ph.D

Dr Gareth Moore is an Ace Puzzler, and author of lots of puzzle books.

He created an online brain-training site called BrainedUp.com, and runs a puzzle site called PuzzleMix.com. Gareth has a Ph.D from the University of Cambridge, where he taught machines to understand spoken English.

Let the
BRAIN
GAMES
begin!

All but one of these pictures are identical, except for their rotation. Can you find the one that is different to the rest? Which picture is the odd one out?

Draw horizontal and vertical lines to join all of the circles into pairs, so that each pair consists of one white and one shaded circle. The lines you draw to join the circles cannot cross each other, and they also can't cross over other circles.

Take a look at this example solution to see how it works:

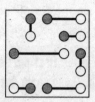

a)

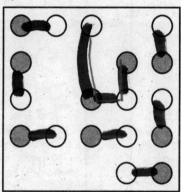

b)

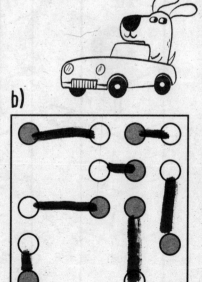

BRAIN GAME 3 →

 TIME ....

Can you solve these brain chains in your head, without writing down any numbers until the final answer?

Start with the value at the top of each puzzle, then follow each arrow in turn and do what the mathematical instructions say until you reach the 'Result' box. Write the final value you have in that box.

For example, in the first puzzle you would start with 5, then multiply by 2, then add 7, and so on until you reach the bottom.

a)
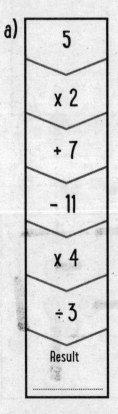

| 5 |
| x 2 |
| + 7 |
| – 11 |
| x 4 |
| ÷ 3 |
| Result |
| .... |

b)
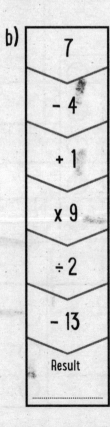

| 7 |
| – 4 |
| + 1 |
| x 9 |
| ÷ 2 |
| – 13 |
| Result |
| .... |

c)
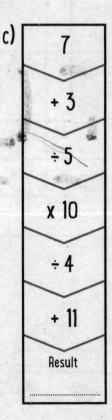

| 7 |
| + 3 |
| ÷ 5 |
| x 10 |
| ÷ 4 |
| + 11 |
| Result |
| .... |

How many separate rectangles can you count in this image by tracing along the lines in various ways? Be careful, since there are more than you might think!

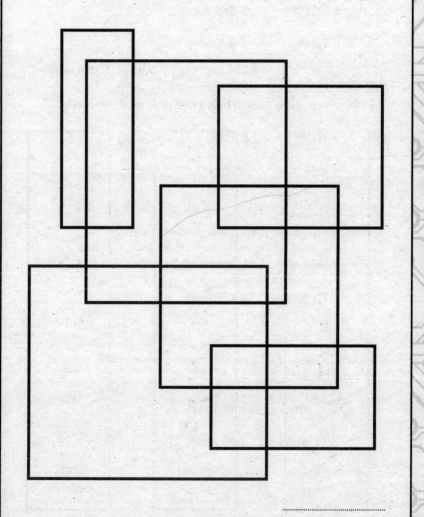

It's quiz time! See how many of the following multiple-choice questions you can answer.

1. Which planet is the largest in our solar system?

    a. Saturn   b. Neptune

    c. Venus   d. Jupiter   ....

2. In what year did a human being first walk on the moon?

    a. 1949   b. 1969

    c. 1989   d. 2009   ....

3. What is the name of the galaxy in which we live?

    a. Milky Way   b. Andromeda

    c. The Plough   d. Cassiopeia   ....

4. How long does it take for the earth to travel once around the sun?

    a. 14 weeks   b. 28 weeks

    c. 47 weeks   d. 52 weeks   ....

These pictures all look the same, but in fact only two of them are identical. Which two?

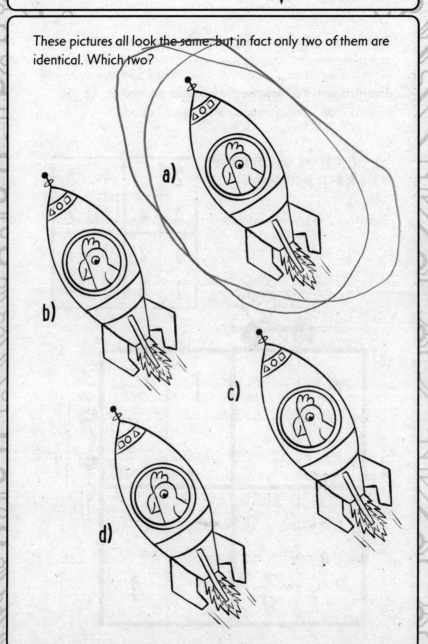

a)

b)

c)

d)

Can you solve each of these sudoku puzzles?

All you need to do is place a number from 1 to 4 into every empty square. You must do this in such a way that no number repeats in any row, column or bold-lined 2x2 box.

Take a look at this example solution to see how the puzzle works:

2	1	4	3
3	4	1	2
4	2	3	1
1	3	2	4

a)

b)

2			
	3		2
4		1	

c)

	2		1
4		2	

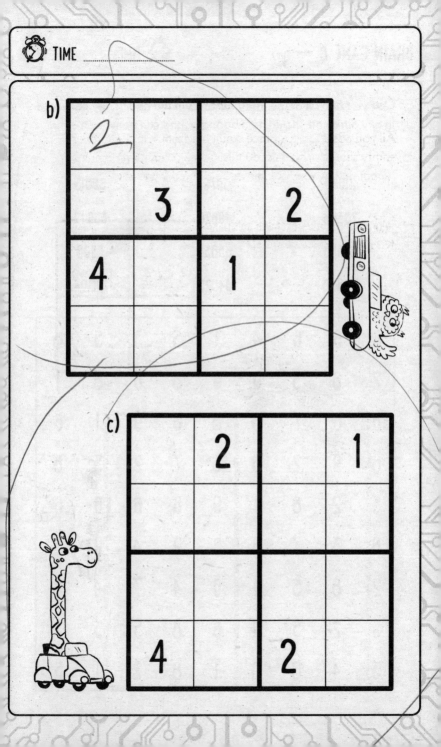

 TIME

Can you find all of the listed numbers in the grid? They can run in any direction, including diagonally, and can be written either forwards or backwards.

21645	39791	65815
28388	49626	66949
32968	63836	7908
38838	64525	81004

6	6	6	4	1	5	3	5	8
2	8	3	9	9	8	6	8	1
8	6	7	8	8	6	9	1	6
8	9	2	3	3	7	2	5	8
3	2	8	1	9	6	6	6	6
8	3	7	6	6	9	4	9	5
2	8	5	1	9	4	7	4	8
5	2	5	4	6	8	5	5	1
3	4	0	0	1	8	2	1	5

You have the following bunch of balloons, each of which has a different number painted on it:

Which balloons would you burst so that the numbers on those remaining add together to form each of the following totals? For example, you could form a total of 11 by bursting all except the 5 and 6 balloons, since 5 + 6 = 11.

Targets:

20 = ...

23 = ...

26 = ...

Can you fill in each of these number pyramids? Each block should contain a number equal to the sum of the two blocks immediately beneath it.

Take a look at this example solution to see how it works:

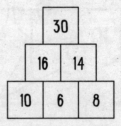

a)

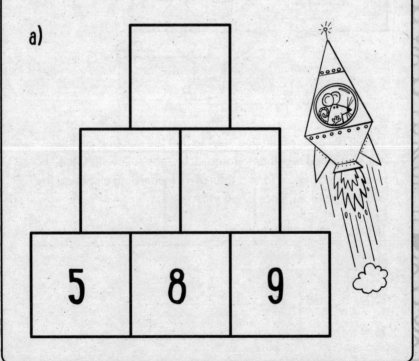

b)

23

12

8

c)

16

7   4

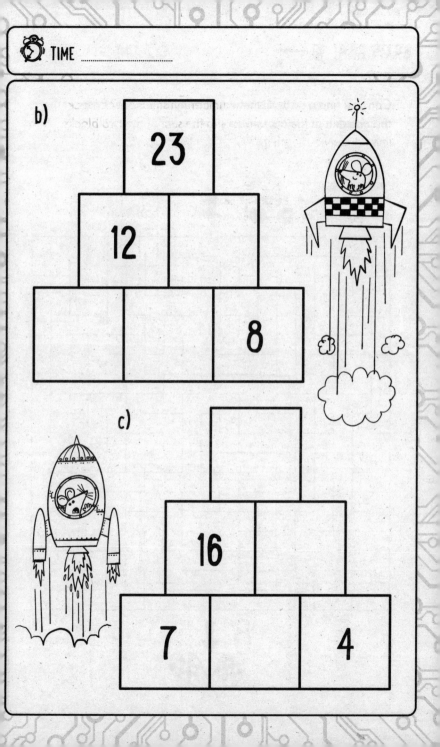

Can you find a path all the way through this maze? Enter at the top and exit at the bottom, as shown.

Take a look at the cars below and spend a minute or two remembering what they look like. Then, when you're ready, turn to the next page where three new cars will have been added.

Can you circle all the new cars?

Can you fill in the empty squares so that each grid contains every number from 1 to 16 once each? There is just one rule, which is that you must be able to start at '1' and then move to '2', '3', '4' and so on by moving only to touching grid squares. You can only move left, right, up and down between squares, but not diagonally.

Take a look at this example solution to see how it works:

10	9	8	1
11	12	7	2
16	13	6	3
15	14	5	4

a)

			1
	8		2
16		10	
15			

b)

		5	
14			3
11			2
	9		

These pictures all look similar, but there are in fact three identical pairs. Can you join the objects into their matching-image pairs?

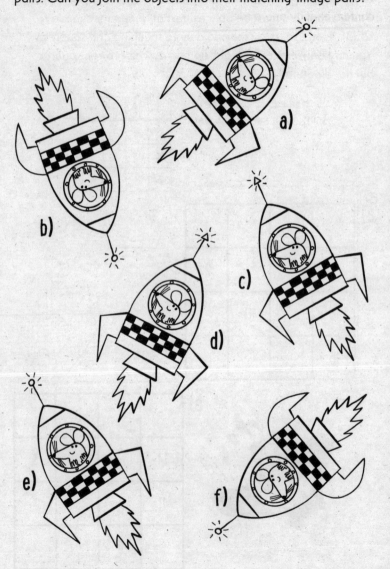

Draw along the dashed lines to divide the grid into squares of various sizes with no unused areas left over. Every square must contain exactly one circle.

Take a look at the example to see how it works:

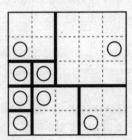

a)

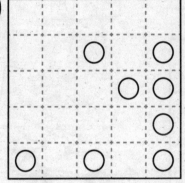

b)

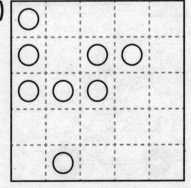

Can you use your powers of deduction to work out which grid squares contain hidden cones in each of these puzzles?

- Any empty grid square can contain a cone, but none of the numbered squares do.

- A number in a square tells you how many cones there are in touching squares, including diagonally touching squares.

Take a look at this example solution to see how it works:

	1	0
▲		1
▲	3	▲

a)

1		
	4	2
	3	

b)

	2	1
2		
	2	1

Can you join all of the dots to form a single loop that visits every dot?

You can only use straight horizontal or vertical lines to join dots, and the loop can't cross or touch itself. Some parts of the loop have already been drawn already to get you started.

Take a look at this example solution to see how it works:

a)

b)

Can you place all of the listed numbers into the grid? Each number can be written either horizontally or vertically, and each number is used exactly once each. They are sorted by length to help you work out which numbers can fit into which gaps.

| 8 | 9 | 5 |

3 DIGITS

229

~~895~~

5 DIGITS

22885

46878

89942

92634

6 DIGITS

915298

982998

7 DIGITS

4255968

6281854

Can you discover what is going on in each of the following numerical sequences, and then work out which number should come next?

For example, if the numbers were 15, 17, 19, 21 and 23 then the sequence would be "add 2 at each step" – so the next number would be 25.

1)   65   55   45   35   25   _____

2)   98   87   76   65   54   _____

3)   14   17   20   23   26   _____

4)   243   81   27   9   3   _____

5)   10   12   15   19   24   _____

Imagine cutting out and folding up this picture, to form a six-sided cube. Which of the options, a) to d), would be the result?

a)

b)

c)

d)

It's quiz time! See how many of the following multiple-choice questions you can answer.

1. On which of these continents can you find Mount Everest, the world's tallest mountain?

      a. Asia   b. Europe

      c. North America d. Africa   ....

2. Stockholm is which European country's capital city?

      a. Norway   b. Finland

      c. Denmark   d. Sweden   ....

3. The Great Barrier Reef, the world's largest coral reef system, can be found off the coast of which of these countries?

      a. Canada   b. Australia

      c. Portugal   d. Madagascar   ....

4. Three of these countries share a border with France. Which one does not?

      a. Spain   b. Italy

      c. Austria   d. Germany   ....

Can you solve each of these sudoku puzzles?

All you need to do is place a number from 1 to 4 into every empty square. You must do this in such a way that no number repeats in any row, column or bold-lined 2x2 box.

Take a look at this example solution to see how the puzzle works:

2	1	4	3
3	4	1	2
4	2	3	1
1	3	2	4

a)

			1
	3		
		2	
2			

b)

2	1		
			2
4			
		2	

c)

	2	1	
	3		
		3	
	1	2	

Can you fill in each of these number pyramids? Each block should contain a number equal to the sum of the two blocks immediately beneath it.

Take a look at this example solution to see how it works:

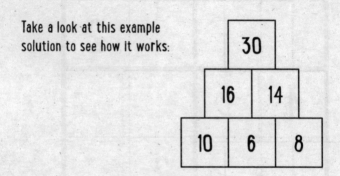

a)

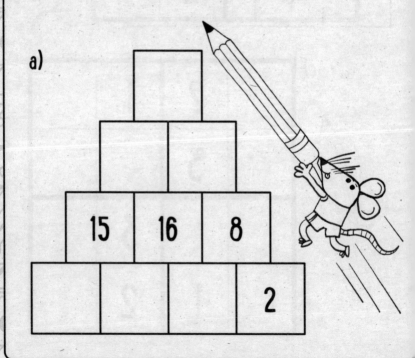

b)

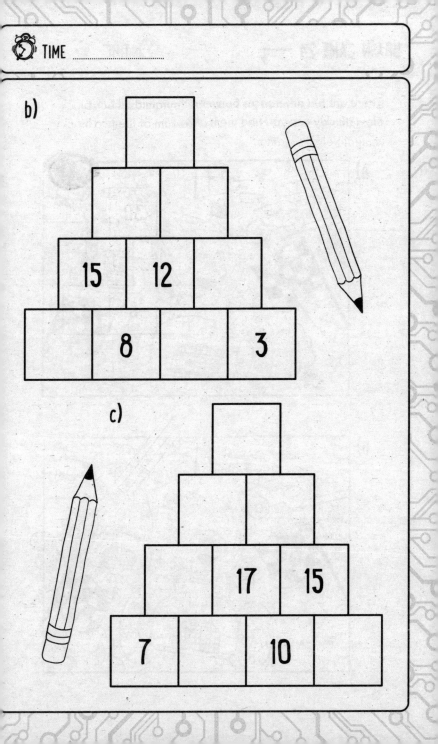

| | |
| 15 | 12 |

| | 8 | | 3 |

c)

| | 17 | 15 |

| 7 | | 10 | |

There are ten differences between these two pictures.
How quickly can you find them all?

a)

b)

For each of these two puzzles, can you draw a loop that visits every white square? The loop can only travel horizontally or vertically between touching squares, and cannot enter any square more than once.

This example solution should help you see how it works:

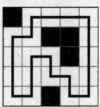

a)

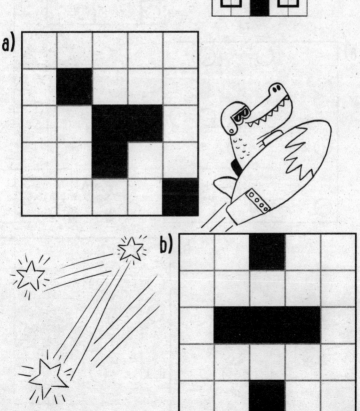

b)

Draw along the dashed lines to divide the grid into squares of various sizes, with no unused areas left over. Every square must contain exactly one circle.

Take a look at the example to see how it works:

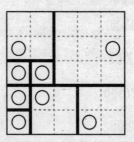

a)

b)

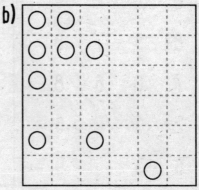

Can you find all of the listed numbers in the grid? They can run in any direction, including diagonally, and can be written either forwards or backwards.

13061	58584	7828
1582	66644	80771
27588	67005	81943
46062	72703	95241

0	3	0	7	2	7	8	1	2
7	6	0	7	7	4	4	8	8
3	7	8	5	8	2	5	8	1
2	0	2	5	5	1	5	7	6
8	0	8	9	4	7	7	6	0
8	5	7	8	2	0	6	8	3
7	0	6	8	8	4	8	1	1
2	6	0	6	4	6	2	4	6
6	5	5	9	3	4	9	1	8

How many building-block cubes have been used to create the picture at the bottom of this page? None of the cubes are floating in mid-air. The picture started off as this 4x4x3 arrangement of 48 cubes before some were removed:

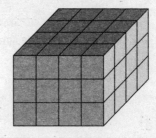

How many cubes are there in this picture?

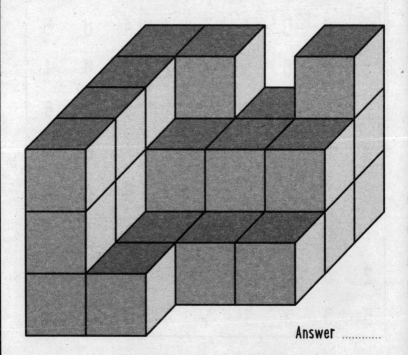

Answer ....

Draw horizontal and vertical lines to join all of the circles into pairs, so that each pair consists of one white and one shaded circle. The lines you draw to join the circles cannot cross each other, and they also can't cross over other circles.

Take a look at this example solution to see how it works:

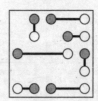

a)

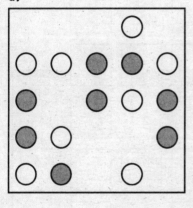

b)

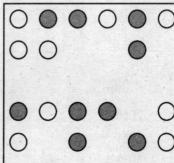

Can you place all of the listed numbers into the grid? Each number can be written either horizontally or vertically, and each number is used exactly once. They are sorted by length to help you work out which numbers can fit into which gaps.

4 DIGITS	5 DIGITS	7 DIGITS
2068	90582	2039870
3881		7205038
5032		8102189
7981		

Take a look at the toys below and spend a minute remembering what they look like. Then, when you're ready, turn to the next page where three of the toys will have been removed. Can you write down the names of those missing toys?

For example, if you think the teddy bear has vanished, write down 'teddy bear'.

Which three toys have vanished?

_____

_____

_____

Can you fill in the empty squares so that each grid contains every number from 1 to 16 once each? There is just one rule, which is that you must be able to start at '1' and then move to '2', '3', '4' and so on by moving only to touching grid squares. You can move left, right, up and down between squares, but not diagonally.

Take a look at this example solution to see how it works:

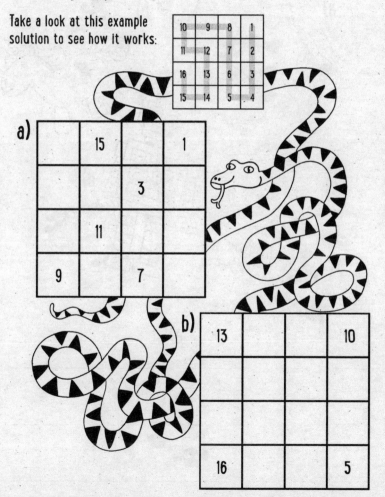

All but one of these pictures are identical, except for their rotation. Can you find the one that is slightly different to the rest? Which picture is the odd one out?

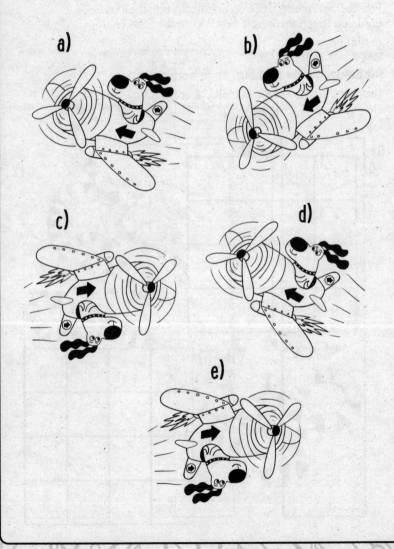

Can you solve these brain chains in your head, without writing down any numbers until the final answer?

Start with the value at the top of each puzzle, then follow each arrow in turn and do what the mathematical instructions say until you reach the 'result' box. Write the final value you have in that box.

For example, in the first puzzle you would start with 20, then add 14, then subtract 18, and so on until you reach the bottom.

a)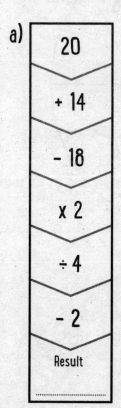

b)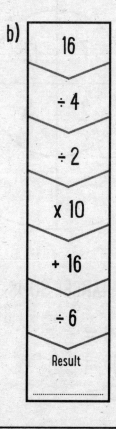

c)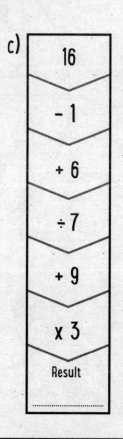

Can you form each of the given sums by choosing one number from both rings of this dartboard and then adding them together?

For example, you could form a sum of 6 by picking 2 from the innermost ring and 4 from the outermost ring.

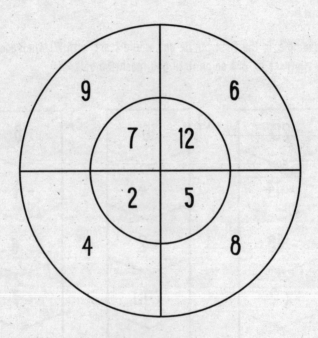

TARGET SUMS:

9 = ...

15 = ...

21 = ...

For both of the following puzzles, can you work out which of the four options shown is most likely to replace the question mark in order to complete the sequence of four images?

Puzzle 1

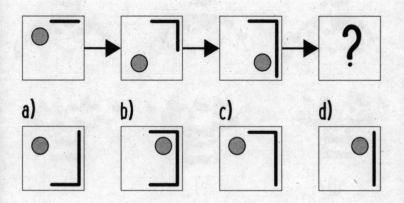

a)   b)   c)   d)

Puzzle 2

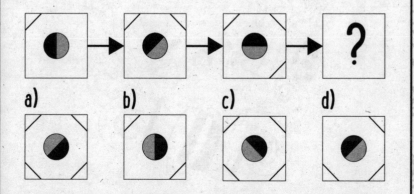

a)   b)   c)   d)

These vases have been cut into two in three different ways.
Can you match each half picture to its corresponding other half?

a)   b)   c)

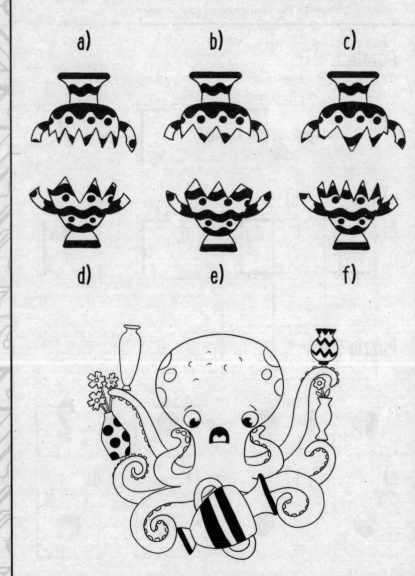

d)   e)   f)

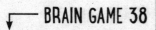
Can you use your powers of deduction to work out which grid squares contain hidden aliens in each of these puzzles?

- Any empty grid square can contain an alien, but none of the numbered squares do.

- A number in a square tells you how many aliens there are in touching squares, including diagonally touching squares.

Take a look at this example solution to see how it works:

	1	0
👽		1
👽	3	👽

a)

2		2
2		2
1	1	

b)

	2		1
	4		2
1			1

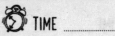

Can you solve these puzzles by placing the numbers 1 to 3 once each into every row and column?

Numbers must obey the arrows, which act as 'greater than' and 'less than' signs. The arrows always point from the bigger number to the smaller number of a pair. This means that, for example, you could have '2 > 1' since 2 is greater than 1, but '1 > 2' would be wrong because 1 is not greater in value than 2.

Take a look at this example
solution to see how it works:

1	2 <	3
	∨	
3	1	2
2	3	1

a)

		> 1
	∧ 3	
2		

b)

2		1
	∧	<

These questions are all about counting days.

1. How many days are there in the period from the 18th December to the 14th January, including both of these dates?

_____

2. If my birthday is on the 1st July and today is the 28th May, how many days is it until my birthday?

_____

3. If today is the 22nd October, what was the date 36 days ago?

_____

4. If my summer holiday lasts from Friday 3rd July to Friday 28th August, how many Wednesdays will there be during the holiday?

_____

5. If today is a Thursday, what day of the week will it be 25 days from now?

_____

Can you solve each of these sudoku puzzles?

All you need to do is place a number from 1 to 6 into every empty square. You must do this in such a way that no number repeats in any row, column or bold-lined 2x3 box.

Take a look at this example solution to see how the puzzle works:

2	5	3	1	4	6
4	6	5	2	1	3
3	1	6	4	2	5
6	4	1	5	3	2
5	2	4	3	6	1
1	3	2	6	5	4

a)

2		5	1		4
		4	6		
4	6			1	5
6	4			2	3
		6	4		
1		2	3		6

b)

	2	1	6	5	
4					6
1		5	4		3
6		3	5		2
2					5
	4	6	2	3	

There's only one piece needed to complete this puzzle, but unfortunately some pieces from other jigsaws have been mixed in with the correct piece. Can you work out which piece should be used to complete the picture?

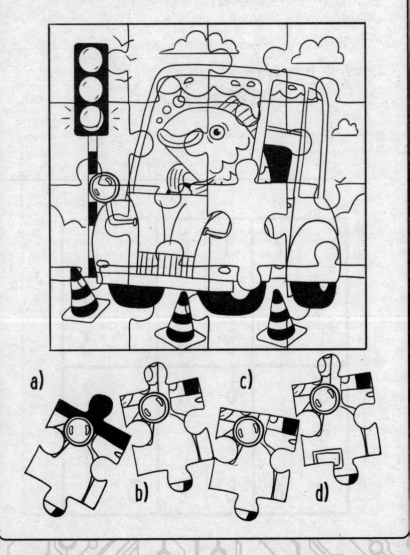

Can you solve these brain chains in your head, without writing down any numbers until the final answer?

Start with the value at the top of each puzzle, then follow each arrow in turn and do what the mathematical instructions say until you reach the 'result' box. Write the final value you have in that box.

For example, in the first puzzle you would start with 16, then divide by 4, then add 3, and so on until you reach the bottom.

a)
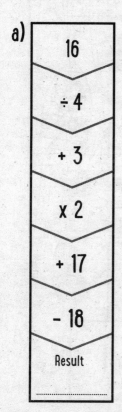

| 16 |
| ÷ 4 |
| + 3 |
| x 2 |
| + 17 |
| − 18 |
| Result |

b)
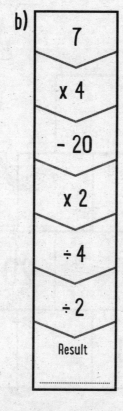

| 7 |
| x 4 |
| − 20 |
| x 2 |
| ÷ 4 |
| ÷ 2 |
| Result |

c)
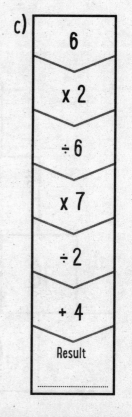

| 6 |
| x 2 |
| ÷ 6 |
| x 7 |
| ÷ 2 |
| + 4 |
| Result |

Can you fill in each of these number pyramids? Each block should contain a number equal to the sum of the two blocks immediately beneath it.

Take a look at this example solution to see how it works:

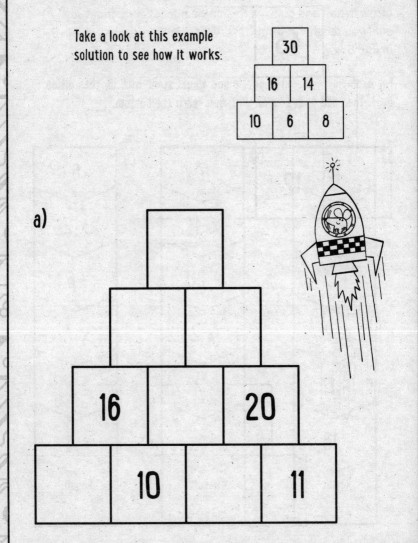

	30	
16		14
10	6	8

a)

16			20	
	10			11

b)

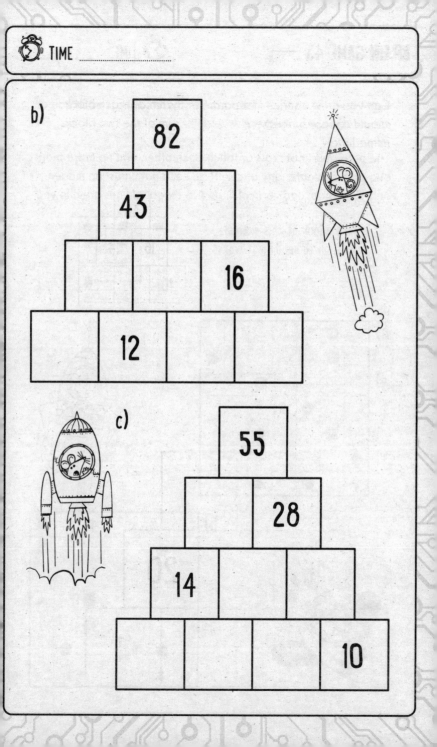

```
        82
    43
         16
    12
```

c)

```
        55
         28
    14
                10
```

Can you draw a series of separate paths to connect each pair of identical shapes together?

The paths must not cross or touch each other, and no more than one path can enter any grid square. Each path must be made up of only horizontal and vertical lines. No diagonal lines are allowed.

Take a look at this example solution to see how it works:

a)

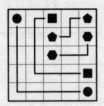

b)

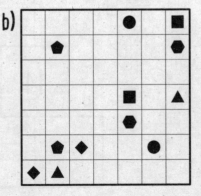

The four grey arrows on this page all represent applying the same rule. Look at the first three rows and work out what rule the arrows represent, then apply the same rule to the fourth row. Which of the options, a) to d), should replace the question mark?

a)

b)

c)

d)

For each of the pictures on the left, which of the three options on the right would be the result if that picture was reflected as if in a vertical mirror?

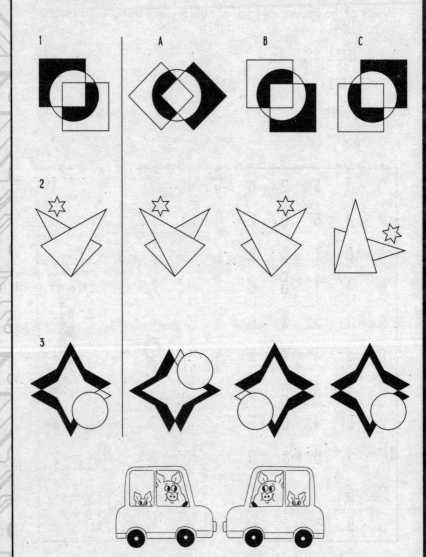

Can you find all of the listed numbers in the grid? They can run in any direction, including diagonally, and can be written either forwards or backwards.

11841	39628	74081
15184	45666	75997
17102	54039	88372
22741	7088	89092
35065	72909	

0	1	5	2	8	7	8	9	2	1	1
8	4	6	0	2	5	9	7	0	4	0
8	8	7	6	6	7	3	9	9	8	4
6	1	1	0	6	8	1	2	5	0	0
9	1	5	2	8	5	5	7	8	7	1
0	3	1	7	5	4	4	4	1	1	4
9	8	8	0	4	4	5	4	8	0	7
2	6	4	0	7	0	0	8	9	6	2
7	2	8	8	0	3	8	3	0	4	2
0	8	1	7	8	7	5	1	9	0	7
3	9	6	2	8	4	6	2	2	0	1

Can you solve each of these sudoku puzzles?

All you need to do is place a number from 1 to 6 into every empty square. You must do this in such a way that no number repeats in any row, column or bold-lined 2x3 box.

Take a look at this example solution to see how the puzzle works:

2	5	3	1	4	6
4	6	5	2	1	3
3	1	6	4	2	5
6	4	1	5	3	2
5	2	4	3	6	1
1	3	2	6	5	4

a)

	2		5		
			1		2
3	5				
				6	1
2		1			
		6		2	

b)

		3	4		
	3			5	
4					6
5					3
	4			2	
		2	3		

Can you solve these puzzles by placing the numbers 1 to 4 once each into every row and column?

Numbers must obey the arrows, which act as 'greater than' and 'less than' signs. The arrows always point from the bigger number to the smaller number of a pair. This means that, for example, you could have '2 > 1' since 2 is greater than 1, but '1 > 2' would be wrong because 1 is not greater in value than 2.

Take a look at this example solution to see how it works:

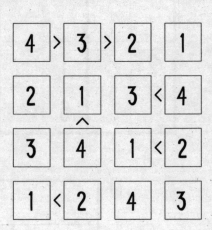

a)

☐ **>**	☐	☐	**1**
∧	**∨**		
☐	☐	**3**	☐
		∨	
☐	**3**	☐	☐
∧	**∧**		
2	☐	☐	☐

b)

3 >	☐	☐	☐
			∧
☐	**4**	☐	☐
		∧	
☐ **<**	☐	**3 <**	☐
		∨	
☐	☐	☐	**1**

Can you match the silhouettes to the planes?

a)

b)

c)

d)

e)

f)

g)

h)

How many separate rectangles can you count in this image by tracing along the lines in various ways? Be careful, since there are more than you might think!

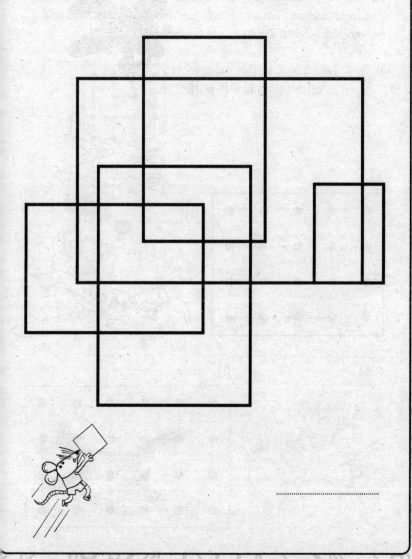

Can you join all of the dots to form a single loop that visits every dot?

You can only use straight horizontal or vertical lines to join dots, and the loop can't cross or touch itself. Some parts of the loop have already been drawn to get you started.

Take a look at this example solution to see how it works:

a)

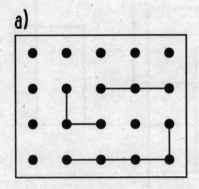

b)

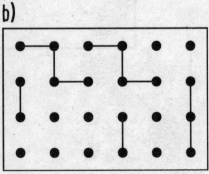

These pictures all look similar, but there are in fact four identical pairs. Can you join the objects into their matching-image pairs?

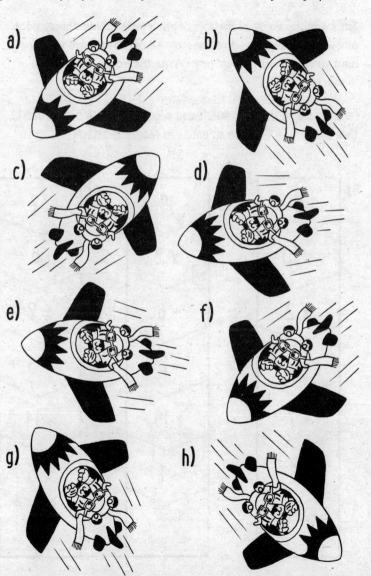

a)

b)

c)

d)

e)

f)

g)

h)

Can you solve these brain chains in your head, without writing down any numbers until the final answer?

Start with the value at the top of each puzzle, then follow each arrow in turn and do what the mathematical instructions say until you reach the 'result' box. Write the final value you have in that box.

For example, in the first puzzle you would start with 5, then add 10, then multiply by 2 and so on until you reach the bottom.

a)

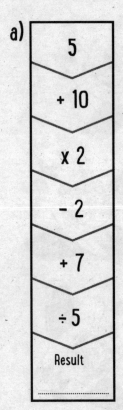

5
+ 10
x 2
- 2
+ 7
÷ 5
Result
....

b)

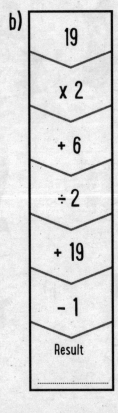

19
x 2
+ 6
÷ 2
+ 19
- 1
Result
....

c)

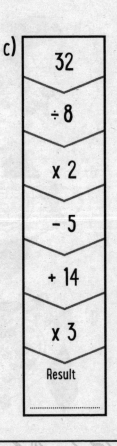

32
÷ 8
x 2
- 5
+ 14
x 3
Result
....

Can you find a path all the way through this twisty maze?
Enter at the top and exit at the bottom, as shown.

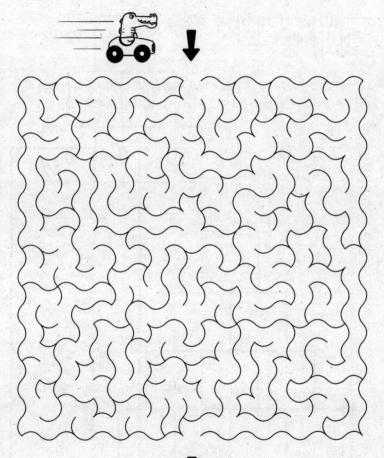

Can you fill in each of these number pyramids? Each block should contain a number equal to the sum of the two blocks immediately beneath it.

Take a look at this example solution to see how it works:

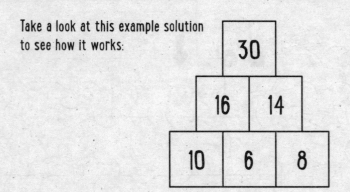

a)

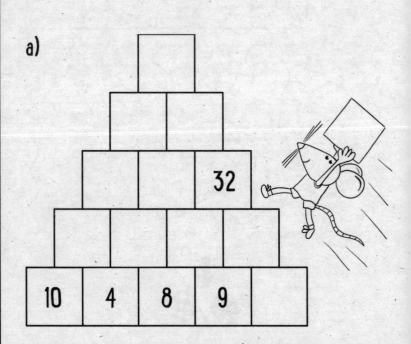

b)

Can you place a letter from A to E into every empty square, so that no letter repeats in any row or column? Identical letters can't be in touching squares — not even diagonally.

Take a look at this example solution to see how it works:

E	A	B	D	C
D	C	E	A	B
A	B	D	C	E
C	E	A	B	D
B	D	C	E	A

a)

E		D		A
		A		
A	E		D	C
		C		
C		E		D

b)

A		B		E
	E		C	
C		D		A
	A		B	
B		E		C

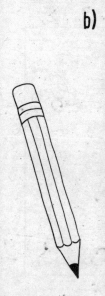

⏱ TIME ....

There are ten differences between these two pictures.
How quickly can you find them all?

Can you find all of the listed numbers in the grid? They can run in any direction, including diagonally, and can be written either forwards or backwards.

12561	23424	71985
12816	25031	80103
20272	25820	80621
21785	28474	81581
22996	31878	

1	2	1	3	2	1	2	8	5	8	3
3	2	3	8	2	1	8	2	1	0	9
9	8	4	2	6	1	6	9	9	2	2
1	7	1	5	5	1	6	2	7	7	5
4	9	2	8	0	2	8	2	6	1	2
7	1	1	2	2	0	0	2	1	9	5
0	5	8	3	2	2	8	5	1	8	2
2	5	4	3	0	5	8	2	2	5	1
2	2	8	0	1	0	3	2	6	5	7
4	0	6	1	2	3	8	2	0	4	8
6	9	8	7	8	1	3	2	8	5	5

Imagine cutting out and folding up this picture, to form a six-sided cube. Which of the options, a) to d), would be the result?

a)

b)

c)

d)

Draw straight lines to join the dots in increasing order of the 3-times table, starting at 3.

Can you find a path all the way through this circular maze?
Enter at the top and exit at the bottom, as shown.

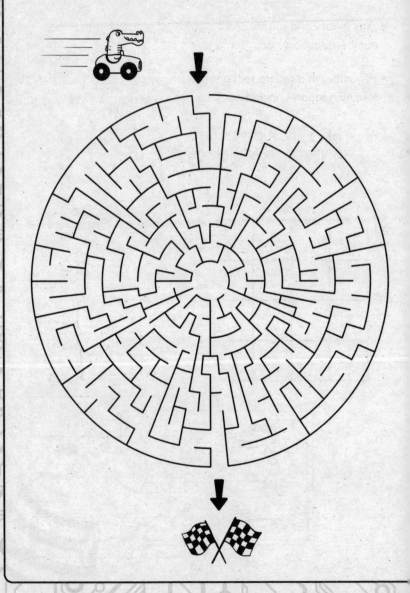

Can you use your powers of deduction to work out which grid squares contain hidden cones in each of these puzzles?

- Any empty grid square can contain a cone, but none of the numbered squares do.

- A number in a square tells you how many cones there are in touching squares, including diagonally touching squares.

Take a look at this example solution to see how it works:

	1	0
🔺		1
🔺	3	🔺

a)

1		2	
	2	3	
2			2
			2

b)

		2	
3	4	3	
	3		2
1			2

The three grey arrows on this page all represent applying the same rule. Look at the first two rows and work out what rule the arrows represent, then apply the same rule to the third row. Which of the options, a) to d), should replace the question mark?

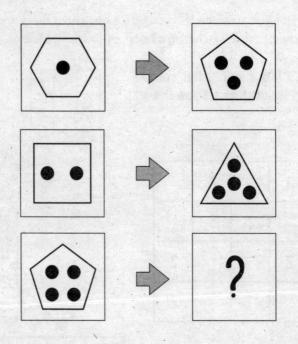

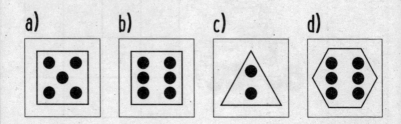

a)   b)   c)   d)

How many building-block cubes have been used to create the picture at the bottom of this page? The picture started off as this 4x4x4 arrangement of 64 cubes before some were removed:

How many cubes are there in this picture?

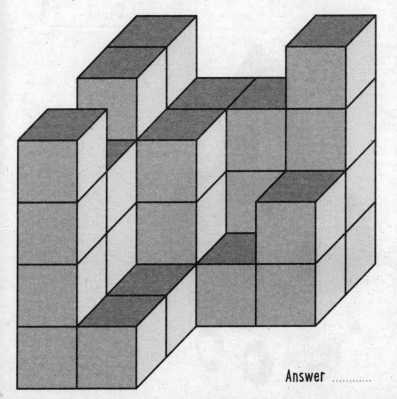

Answer ....

Can you place a letter from A to E into every empty square, so that no letter repeats in any row or column? Identical letters can't be in touching squares — not even diagonally.

Take a look at this example solution to see how it works:

E	A	B	D	C
D	C	E	A	B
A	B	D	C	E
C	E	A	B	D
B	D	C	E	A

a)

A				D
		D		
	A		C	
		B		
B				C

b)

	D		B	
A				D
D				C
	E		D	

For both of the following puzzles, can you work out which of the four options shown is most likely to replace the question mark in order to complete the sequence of four images?

Puzzle 1

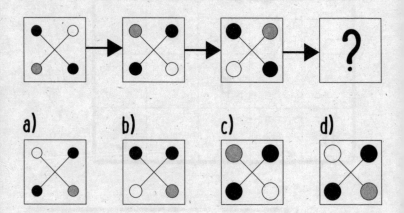

Puzzle 2

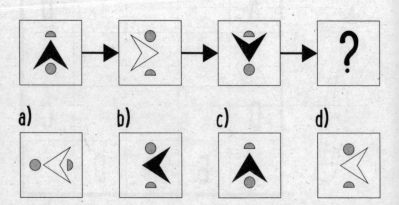

Can you find a path all the way through this angular maze?
Enter at the top and exit at the bottom, as shown.

For each of these two puzzles, can you draw a loop that visits every white square? The loop can only travel horizontally or vertically between touching squares, and cannot enter any square more than once.

This example solution should help you see how it works:

a)

b)

Can you find the five dominoes that complete this circuit? Place one of the loose dominoes on to each shaded domino in order to complete the loop, but without using any of the dominoes more than once. Dominoes can only touch one another if they have the same number of spots on the touching ends. Two of the loose dominoes will be left over.

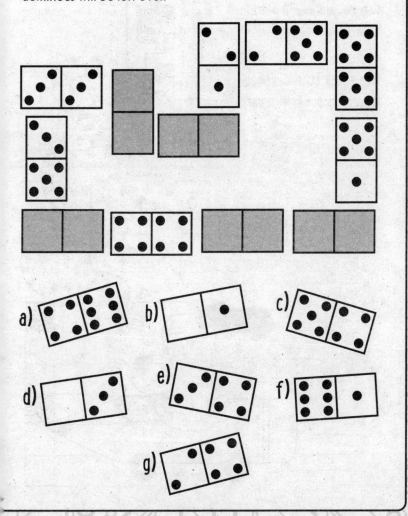

Can you solve these puzzles by placing the numbers 1 to 4 once each into every row and column?

Numbers must obey the arrows, which act as 'greater than' and 'less than' signs. The arrows always point from the bigger number to the smaller number of a pair. This means that, for example, you could have '2 > 1' since 2 is greater than 1, but '1 > 2' would be wrong because 1 is not greater in value than 2.

Take a look at this example solution to see how it works:

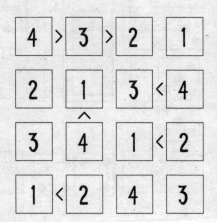

a)

3		>		

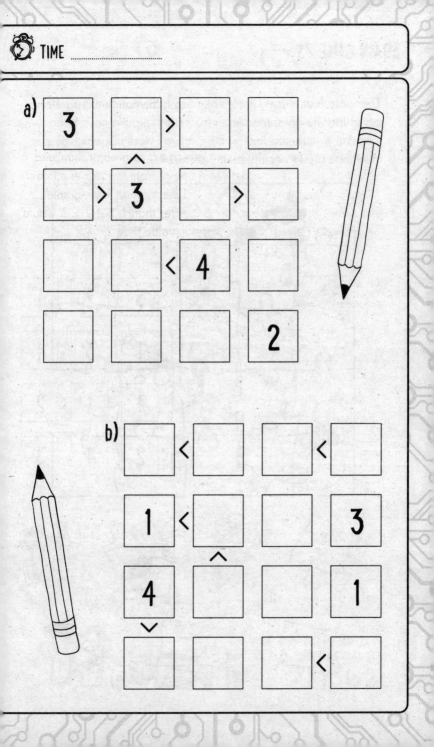

There are four missing pieces needed to complete this puzzle, but unfortunately some pieces from other jigsaws have been mixed in with the correct piece. Can you work out which pieces should be used to complete the picture?

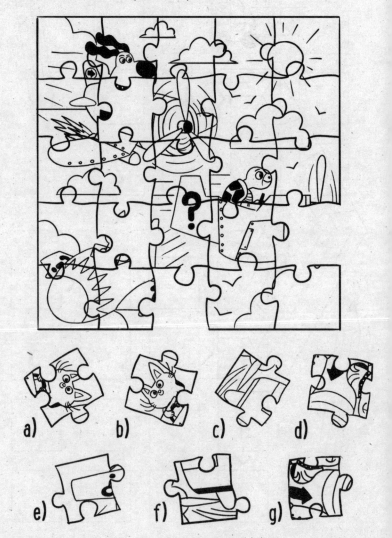

a)   b)   c)   d)

e)   f)   g)

Can you find a path all the way through this hexagonal maze?
Enter at the top and exit at the bottom, as shown.

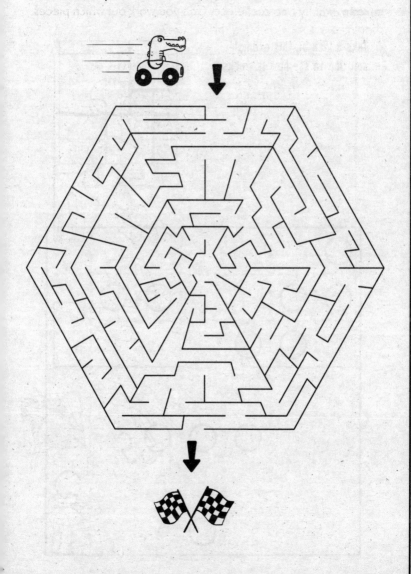

Draw along the dashed lines to divide the grid into squares of various sizes, with no unused areas left over. Every square must contain exactly one circle.

Take a look at this example solution to see how it works:

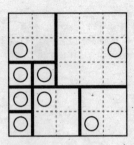

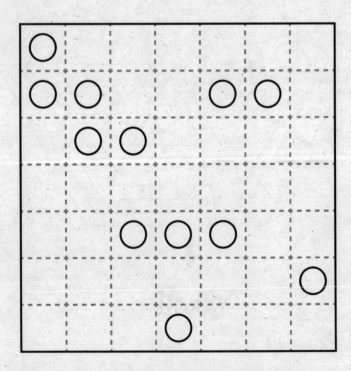

Draw horizontal and vertical lines to join all of the circles into pairs, so that each pair consists of one white and one shaded circle. The lines you draw to join the circles cannot cross each other, and they also can't cross over other circles.

Take a look at this example solution to see how it works:

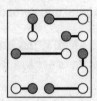

a)

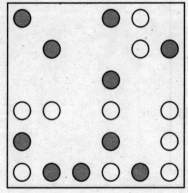

b)

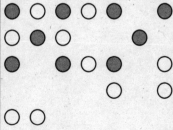

⏰ TIME ....

Can you draw a series of separate paths to connect each pair of identical shapes together?

The paths must not cross or touch each other, and no more than one path can enter any grid square. Each path must be made up of only horizontal and vertical lines. No diagonal lines are allowed.

Take a look at this example solution to see how it works:

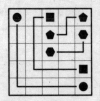

a)

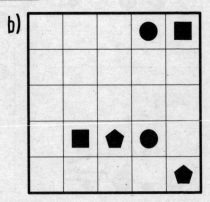

Can you place all of the listed numbers into the grid? Each number can be written either horizontally or vertically, and each number is used exactly once each. They are sorted by length to help you work out which numbers can fit into which gaps.

3 DIGITS

111	491
139	541
272	808
402	935

4 DIGITS

1149
1207
4246
4739

5 DIGITS

11095
28130
38059
86525

7 DIGITS

1382187
2531821
4838339
9101955

Can you join all of the dots to form a single loop that visits every dot?

You can only use straight horizontal or vertical lines to join dots, and the loop can't cross or touch itself. Some parts of the loop have been drawn already to get you started.

Take a look at this example solution to see how it works:

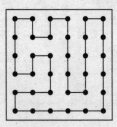

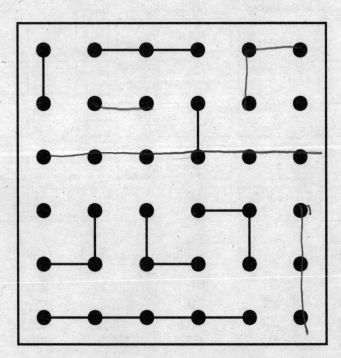

It's quiz time! See how many of the following multiple-choice questions you can answer.

1. How many players are there on a soccer team, not including substitutes?

        a. 9   b. 11

        c. 13   d. 15   ....

2. Which of these sports involves hitting a puck?

        a. Ice hockey   b. Table tennis

        c. Lacrosse   d. Rounders   ....

3. In which modern country did the ancient Olympic Games take place?

        a. Italy   b. Spain

        c. Greece   d. Portugal   ....

4. How many rings are there in the Olympic logo?

        a. 3 rings   b. 5 rings

        c. 7 rings   d. 9 rings   ....

For each of these two puzzles, can you draw a loop that visits every white square? The loop can only travel horizontally or vertically between touching squares, and cannot enter any square more than once.

This example solution should help you see how it works:

a)

b)

Can you draw a series of separate paths to connect each pair of identical shapes together?

The paths must not cross or touch each other, and no more than one path can enter any grid square. Each path must be made up of only horizontal and vertical lines. No diagonal lines are allowed.

Take a look at this example solution to see how it works:

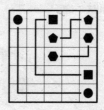

a)

b)

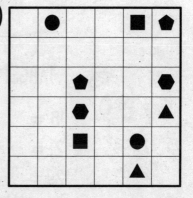

Can you form each of the given sums by choosing one number from each ring of this dartboard and then adding them all together?

For example, you could form a sum of 13 by picking 8 from the innermost ring, 2 from the middle ring and 3 from the outermost ring.

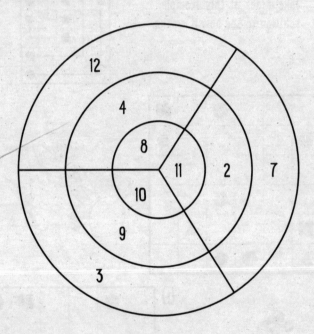

TARGET SUMS:

18 = ...

21 = ...

29 = ...

Can you discover what is going on in each of the following numerical sequences, and then work out which number should come next?

For example, if the numbers were 15, 17, 19, 21 and 23 then the sequence would be "add 2 at each step" – so the next number would be 25.

1)   83   78   73   68   63   58   _____

2)   1   2   4   8   16   32   _____

3)   989   878   767   656   545   434   _____

4)   4   5   9   14   23   37   _____

5)   1   4   9   16   25   36   _____

For each of the pictures on the left, which of the three options on the right would result if that picture was reflected in a vertical mirror?

1   A   B   C

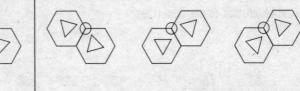

2

3

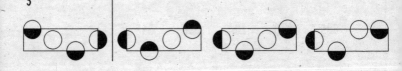

Draw horizontal and vertical lines to join all of the circles into pairs, so that each pair consists of one white and one shaded circle. The lines you draw to join the circles cannot cross each other, and they also can't cross over other circles.

Take a look at this example solution to see how it works:

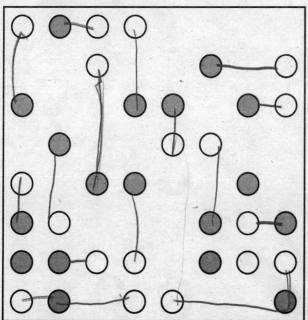

Can you place all of the listed numbers into the grid? Each number can be written either horizontally or vertically, and each number is used exactly once each. They are sorted by length to help you work out which numbers can fit into which gaps.

3 DIGITS	4 DIGITS	5 DIGITS	7 DIGITS
140	3196	30860	7803445
145	3263	49305	9075255
248	3648		
322	7096		
414			
461			
467			
530			
608			
637			
681			
738			
880			
926			

For each of these two puzzles, can you draw a loop that visits every white square? The loop can only travel horizontally or vertically between touching squares, and cannot enter any square more than once.

This example solution should help you see how it works:

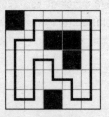

a)

b)

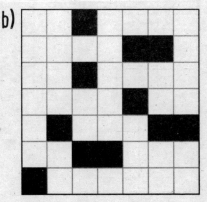

Can you place a letter from A to F into every empty square, so that no letter repeats in any row or column? Identical letters can't be in touching squares – not even diagonally.

Take a look at this example solution to see how it works:

D	B	C	F	E	A
C	F	E	A	D	B
A	D	B	C	F	E
F	E	A	D	B	C
B	C	F	E	A	D
E	A	D	B	C	F

		A	E		
	D			C	
F					E
D					C
	C			E	
		D	C		

Can you form each of the given sums by choosing one number from each ring of this dartboard and then adding them all together?

For example, you could form a sum of 9 by picking 2 from the innermost ring, 4 from the middle ring and 3 from the outermost ring.

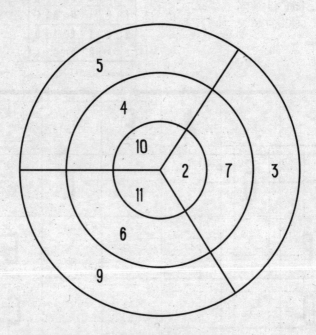

TARGET SUMS:

12 = ...

15 = ...

25 = ...

Can you fill in the empty squares so that each grid contains every number from 1 to 25 once each? There is just one rule, which is that you must be able to start at '1' and then move to '2', '3', '4' and so on by moving only to touching grid squares. You can move left, right, up and down between squares, but not diagonally.

Take a look at this example solution to see how it works:

1	6	7	14	15
2	5	8	13	16
3	4	9	12	17
24	23	10	11	18
25	22	21	20	19

a)

21	22	23	24	
	18		14	
	4	3	2	1

b)

7				
8			19	
9		17		23
	1			24
				25

It's quiz time! See how many of the following multiple-choice questions you can answer.

1. Which of these oceans is the largest in the world?

      a. Indian   b. Atlantic

      c. Pacific   d. Arctic   ....

2. Which of these marine animals is a type of fish?
   The others are all mammals.

      a. Whale   b. Dolphin

      c. Shark   d. Seal   ....

3. Which of these animals makes its own light to attract food?

      a. Anglerfish   b. Sea turtle

      c. Barracuda   d. Stingray   ....

4. Which of these sea creatures can squirt ink to scare
   predators away?

      a. Squid   b. Walrus

      c. Giant clam   d. Pufferfish   ....

Can you match each of these images with its correct silhouette?

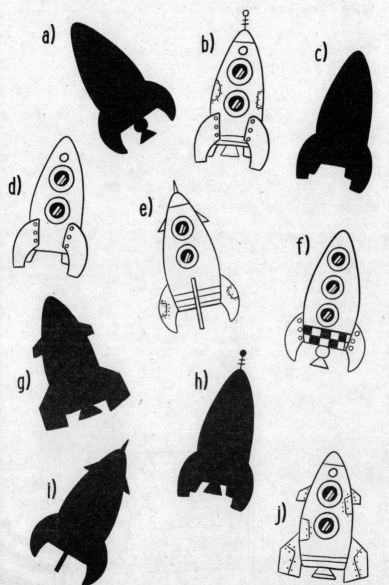

Draw straight lines to join the dots in increasing order
of the 7-times table, starting at 7.

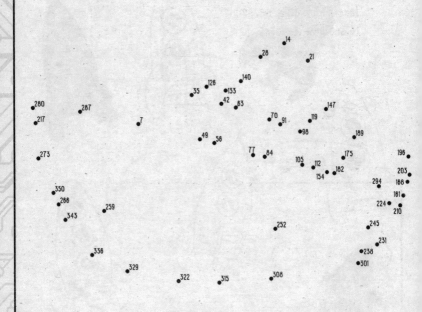

Draw along the dashed lines to divide the grid into squares of various sizes, with no unused areas left over. Every square must contain exactly one circle.

Take a look at the example to see how it works:

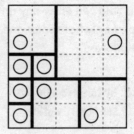

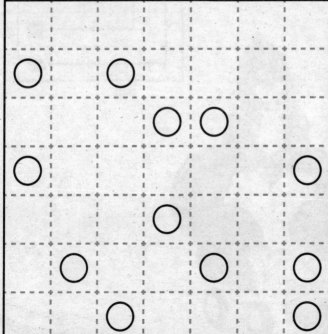

Can you draw a series of separate paths to connect each pair of identical shapes together?

The paths must not cross or touch each other, and no more than one path can enter any grid square. Each path must be made up of only horizontal and vertical lines. No diagonal lines are allowed.

Take a look at this example solution to see how it works:

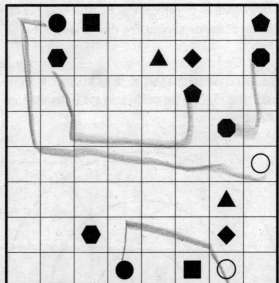

a)

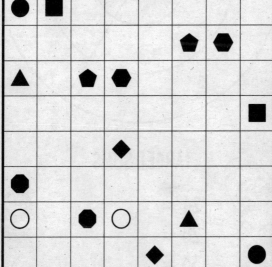

b)

⏱ TIME ....

Can you form each of the given sums by choosing one number from each ring of this dartboard and then adding them all together?

For example, you could form a sum of 16 by picking 7 from the innermost ring, 3 from the middle ring and 6 from the outermost ring.

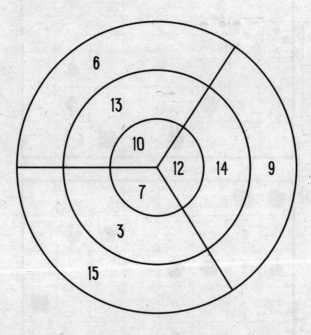

TARGET SUMS:

24 = ...

28 = ...

33 = ...

Can you find the seven dominoes that complete this circuit?
Place one of the loose dominoes on to each shaded domino
in order to complete the loop, but without using any of the
dominoes more than once. Dominoes can only touch one
another if they have the same number of spots on the touching
ends. Which three dominoes will be left over?

You have the following bunch of balloons, each of which has a different number painted on it:

Which balloons would you burst so that the numbers on those remaining add together to form each of the following totals? For example, you could form a total of 17 by bursting all except the 7 and 10 balloons, since 7 + 10 = 17.

Targets:

22 = ...

26 = ...

30 = ...

This picture has been cut into two in four different ways.
Can you match each half picture to its corresponding other half?

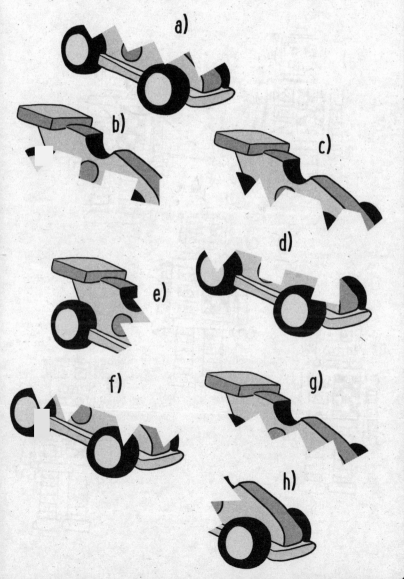

These pictures all look the same, but in fact only two of them are identical. Which two?

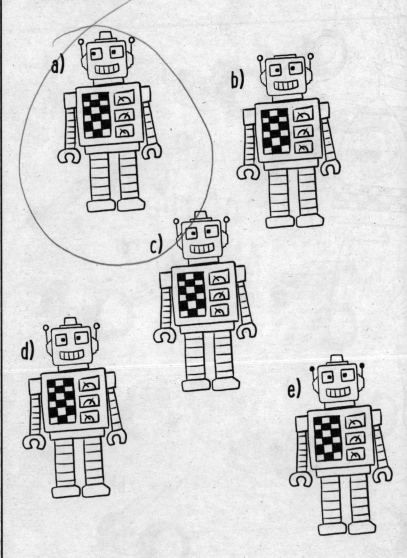

All
of the
ANSWERS

BRAIN GAME 1

The different image is C.

BRAIN GAME 2

a)
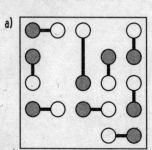

b)
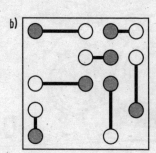

BRAIN GAME 3

a)
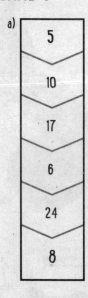

| 5 |
| 10 |
| 17 |
| 6 |
| 24 |
| 8 |

b)
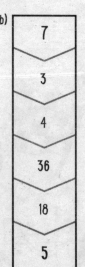

| 7 |
| 3 |
| 4 |
| 36 |
| 18 |
| 5 |

c)
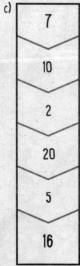

| 7 |
| 10 |
| 2 |
| 20 |
| 5 |
| 16 |

BRAIN GAME 4

There are 25 rectangles to be found.

BRAIN GAME 5

1.   d. Jupiter

2.   b. 1969

3.   a. Milky Way

4.   d. 52 weeks

BRAIN GAME 6

B and C

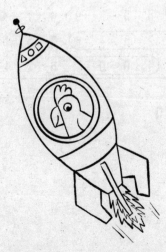

BRAIN GAME 7

a)

4	2	1	3
3	1	4	2
2	4	3	1
1	3	2	4

b)

2	4	3	1
1	3	4	2
4	2	1	3
3	1	2	4

c)

3	2	4	1
1	4	3	2
2	3	1	4
4	1	2	3

BRAIN GAME 8

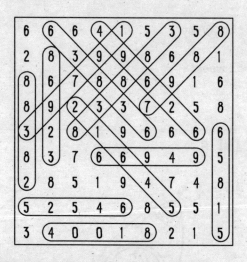

BRAIN GAME 9

20: Burst 10, 6 and 7.

23: Burst 15 and 5.

26: Burst 10 and 7.

BRAIN GAME 10

a)

```
        30
    13      17
  5     8      9
```

b)

```
        23
    12      11
  9     3      8
```

c)

```
        29
    16      13
  7     9      4
```

BRAIN GAME 11

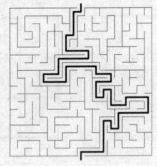

BRAIN GAME 12

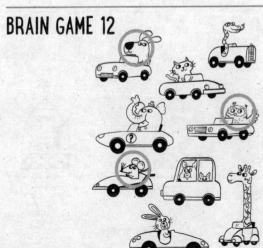

BRAIN GAME 13

a)

6	5	4	1
7	8	3	2
16	9	10	11
15	14	13	12

b)

15	16	5	4
14	13	6	3
11	12	7	2
10	9	8	1

BRAIN GAME 14

a and e   b and f   c and d

BRAIN GAME 15

a)

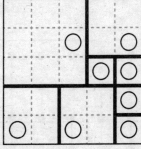

b)

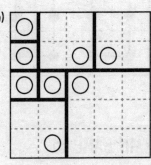

BRAIN GAME 16

a)

1		🔺
🔺	4	2
🔺	3	🔺

b)

🔺	2	1
2		🔺
🔺	2	1

BRAIN GAME 17

a)
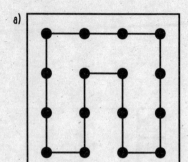

b)
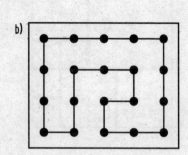

BRAIN GAME 18

9	2	6	3	4		
8		2		2	2	9
2	2	8	8	5		1
9		1		5		5
9		8	9	9	4	2
8	9	5		6		9
		4	6	8	7	8

BRAIN GAME 19

1) 15 – subtract 10 at each step

2) 43 – subtract 11 at each step

3) 29 – add 3 at each step

4) 1 – divide by 3 at each step

5) 30 – add 2, 3, 4, 5, 6 etc. at each step

BRAIN GAME 20

The answer is Cube A. Cubes B and D have sides that do not appear in the picture, while in Cube C the two crossed arrows are not pointing in the correct direction.

BRAIN GAME 21

1. a. Asia

2. d. Sweden

3. b. Australia

4. c. Austria

BRAIN GAME 22

a)

4	2	3	1
1	3	4	2
3	1	2	4
2	4	1	3

b)

2	1	4	3
3	4	1	2
4	2	3	1
1	3	2	4

c)

4	2	1	3
1	3	4	2
2	4	3	1
3	1	2	4

BRAIN GAME 23

a)

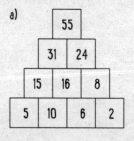

b)

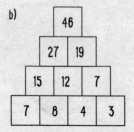

c)

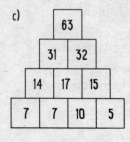

BRAIN GAME 24

BRAIN GAME 25

a)
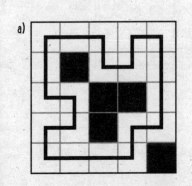

b)
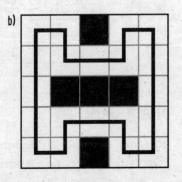

BRAIN GAME 26

a)

b)

BRAIN GAME 27

BRAIN GAME 28

30 cubes – 6 cubes on the top layer, 10 cubes on the middle layer and 14 cubes on the bottom layer.

BRAIN GAME 29

a)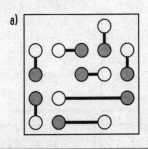

b)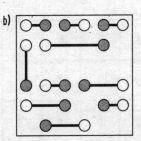

BRAIN GAME 30

2		7	9	8	1
5	0	3	2		1
3		0		0	
9	0	5	8	2	
8		0		1	
7		3	8	8	1
2	0	6	8		9

BRAIN GAME 31

The toys that were removed were:

BRAIN GAME 32

a)

14	15	16	1
13	12	3	2
10	11	4	5
9	8	7	6

b)

13	12	11	10
14	1	8	9
15	2	7	6
16	3	4	5

BRAIN GAME 33

b)

BRAIN GAME 34

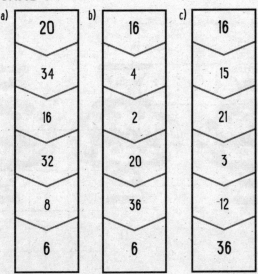

a)

| 20 |
| 34 |
| 16 |
| 32 |
| 8 |
| 6 |

b)

| 16 |
| 4 |
| 2 |
| 20 |
| 36 |
| 6 |

c)

| 16 |
| 15 |
| 21 |
| 3 |
| 12 |
| 36 |

BRAIN GAME 35

$9 = 5 + 4$
$15 = 7 + 8$
$21 = 12 + 9$

BRAIN GAME 36

Puzzle 1
b. At each step the grey circle moves anticlockwise around the box, and another segment of the solid black line is added.

Puzzle 2
c. At each step the central circle rotates 45 degrees clockwise, and a diagonal line is added to another corner while working in a clockwise direction.

BRAIN GAME 37

b)   a)   c)

e)   f)   d)

BRAIN GAME 38

a)

2	🐝	2
2	🐝	2
1	1	

b)

🐝	2	🐝	1
	4		2
1	🐝	🐝	1

BRAIN GAME 39

a)

3	2 >	1
1	3	2
2	1	3

(with ^ between 2 and 3 in first column)

b)

2	3	1
3	1	2
1	2 <	3

(with ^ between 1 and 2 in middle column)

BRAIN GAME 40

1. There are 28 days in the period.

2. It's 34 days until my birthday.

3. The date was the 16th September.

4. There will be 8 Wednesdays.

5. It will be a Monday.

BRAIN GAME 41

a)

2	3	5	1	6	4
5	1	4	6	3	2
4	6	3	2	1	5
6	4	1	5	2	3
3	2	6	4	5	1
1	5	2	3	4	6

b)

3	2	1	6	5	4
4	5	2	3	1	6
1	6	5	4	2	3
6	1	3	5	4	2
2	3	4	1	6	5
5	4	6	2	3	1

BRAIN GAME 42

BRAIN GAME 43

a)

| 16 |
| 4 |
| 7 |
| 14 |
| 31 |
| 13 |

b)

| 7 |
| 28 |
| 8 |
| 16 |
| 4 |
| 2 |

c)

| 6 |
| 12 |
| 2 |
| 14 |
| 7 |
| 11 |

BRAIN GAME 44

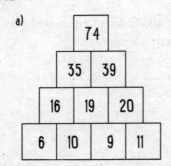

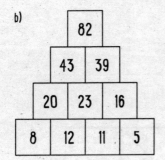

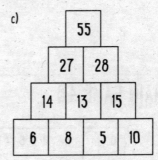

BRAIN GAME 45

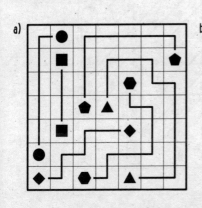

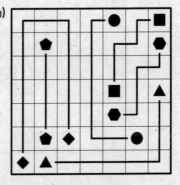

BRAIN GAME 46

D. The rule is that one additional star is shaded grey, and the inner square is rotated by 45 degrees.

BRAIN GAME 47

1.   C

2.   B

3.   B

BRAIN GAME 48

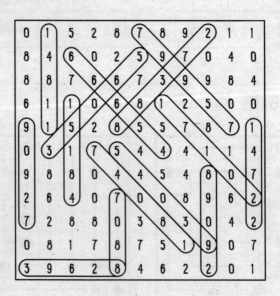

BRAIN GAME 49

a)

1	2	4	5	3	6
6	4	3	1	5	2
3	5	2	6	1	4
4	3	5	2	6	1
2	6	1	3	4	5
5	1	6	4	2	3

b)

6	5	3	4	1	2
2	3	1	6	5	4
4	1	5	2	3	6
5	2	4	1	6	3
3	4	6	5	2	1
1	6	2	3	4	5

BRAIN GAME 50

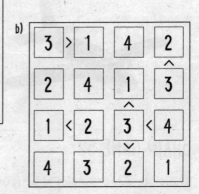

a)

3 >	2	4	1
4	1	3	2
1	3	2	4
2	4	1	3

b)

3 >	1	4	2
2	4	1	3
1 <	2	3 <	4
4	3	2	1

BRAIN GAME 51

a and g

b and c

h and d

e and f

BRAIN GAME 52

There are 22 rectangles to be found.

BRAIN GAME 53

a)

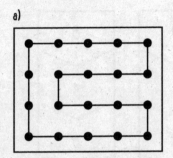

b)

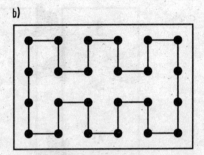

BRAIN GAME 54

a and h

b and e

c and f

d and g

BRAIN GAME 55

a)
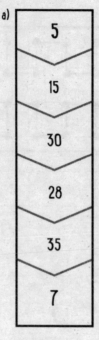

5
15
30
28
35
7

b)
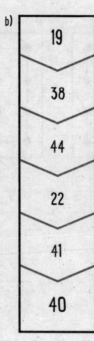

19
38
44
22
41
40

c)
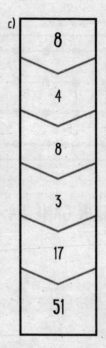

8
4
8
3
17
51

BRAIN GAME 56

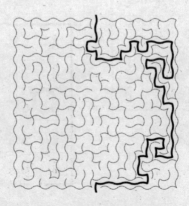

BRAIN GAME 57

a)

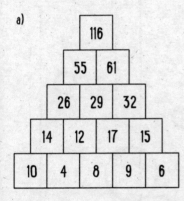

b)

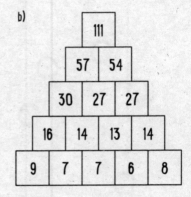

BRAIN GAME 58

a)

E	B	D	C	A
D	C	A	E	B
A	E	B	D	C
B	D	C	A	E
C	A	E	B	D

b)

A	C	B	D	E
D	E	A	C	B
C	B	D	E	A
E	A	C	B	D
B	D	E	A	C

BRAIN GAME 59

BRAIN GAME 60

```
1  2  1  3  2  1  2  8  5  8  3
3  2  3  8  2  1  8  2  1  0  9
9  8  4  2  6  1  6  9  9  2  2
1  7  1  5  5  1  6  2  7  7  5
4  9  2  8  0  2  8  2  6  1  2
7  1  1  2  2  0  0  2  1  9  5
0  5  8  3  2  2  8  5  1  8  2
2  5  4  3  0  5  8  2  2  5  1
2  2  8  0  1  0  3  2  6  5  7
4  0  6  1  2  3  8  2  0  4  8
6  9  8  7  8  1  3  2  8  5  5
```

BRAIN GAME 61

Cube B is the correct result. Cube A has a side that does not appear in the picture; cube C has the striped side and the smiley face the wrong way around; and cube D has the side with five dots and the '+' side the wrong way around.

BRAIN GAME 62

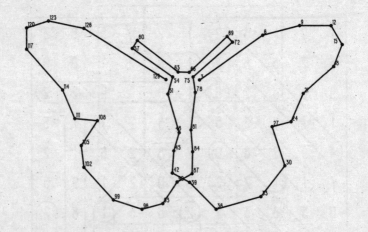

BRAIN GAME 63

BRAIN GAME 64

a)

1	(cone)	2	(cone)
	2	3	
2		(cone)	2
(cone)	(cone)	(cone)	2

b)

(cone)	(cone)	2	(cone)
3	4	3	
(cone)	3	(cone)	2
1		(cone)	2

BRAIN GAME 65

b. The rule is that the number of sides on the polygon is reduced by 1, and two extra black dots are added.

BRAIN GAME 66

33 cubes – 4 cubes on the top layer, 8 cubes on the second layer down, 9 layers on the third layer down, and 12 cubes on the bottom layer.

BRAIN GAME 67

a)

A	E	C	B	D
C	B	D	A	E
D	A	E	C	B
E	C	B	D	A
B	D	A	E	C

b)

C	D	A	B	E
A	B	E	C	D
E	C	D	A	B
D	A	B	E	C
B	E	C	D	A

BRAIN GAME 68

Puzzle 1

d. At each step the four circles all increase in size, and the entire image rotates 90 degrees clockwise.

Puzzle 2

d. At each step the central arrow rotates 90 degrees clockwise and changes between black and white, and the circle and semicircle switch positions.

BRAIN GAME 69

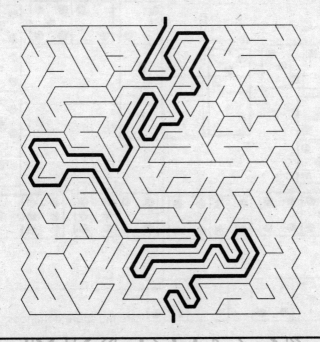

BRAIN GAME 70

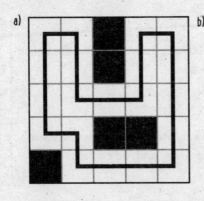

a)

b)

BRAIN GAME 71

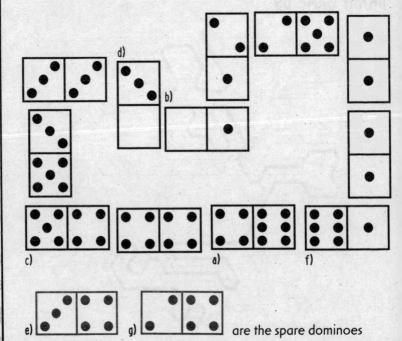

c)

d)

b)

a)

f)

e)

g)

are the spare dominoes

BRAIN GAME 72

a)

3	2 > 1	4

4 > 3	2 > 1

2	1 < 4	3

1	4	3	2

b)

3 < 4	1 < 2

1 < 2	4	3

4	3	2	1

2	1	3 < 4

BRAIN GAME 73

BRAIN GAME 74

BRAIN GAME 75

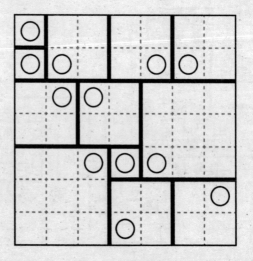

BRAIN GAME 76

a)
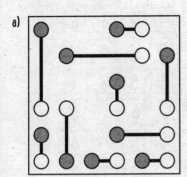

b)
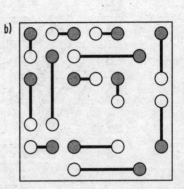

BRAIN GAME 77

a)
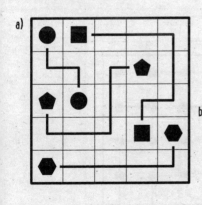

b)
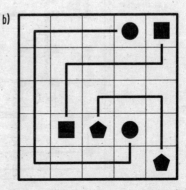

BRAIN GAME 78

4	7	3	9		4	2	4	6
8			3		9		0	
3		2	5	3	1	8	2	1
8	0	8		8		6		3
3		1	1	0	9	5		8
3		3		5		2	7	2
9	1	0	1	9	5	5		1
	1		3		4			8
1	1	4	9		1	2	0	7

BRAIN GAME 79

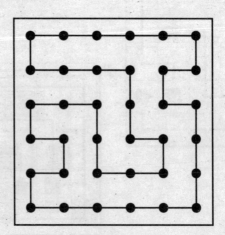

BRAIN GAME 80

1.   b. 11

2.   a. Ice hockey

3.   c. Greece

4.   b. 5 rings

BRAIN GAME 81

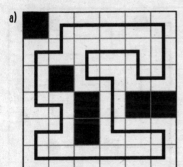

a)

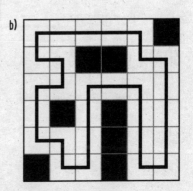

b)

BRAIN GAME 82

a)

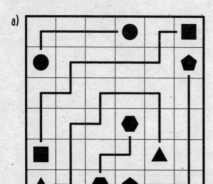

b)

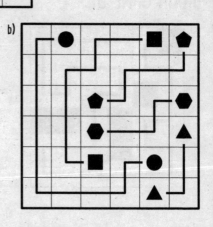

BRAIN GAME 83

$18 = 11 + 4 + 3$

$21 = 10 + 4 + 7$

$29 = 8 + 9 + 12$

BRAIN GAME 84

1) 53 – subtract 5 at each step

2) 64 – multiply by 2 at each step

3) 323 – subtract 111 at each step

4) 60 – add the previous two numbers at each step

5) 49 – the sequence is 1x1, 2x2, 3x3, 4x4, 5x5, 6x6

BRAIN GAME 85

1. C

2. A

3. B

BRAIN GAME 86

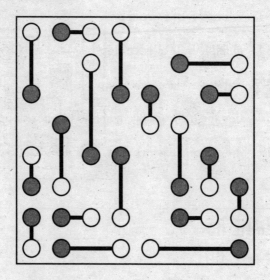

BRAIN GAME 87

6	3	7		3	2	6	3
8		8		6			2
1	4	0		4		9	2	6
		3	0	8	6	0		0
4	1	4				7	3	8
6		4	9	3	0	5
1	4	5		1		2	4	8
	6			9		5		8
	7	0	9	6		5	3	0

BRAIN GAME 88

a)

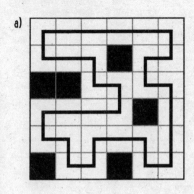

b)

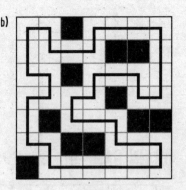

BRAIN GAME 89

C	F	A	E	D	B
E	D	B	F	C	A
F	A	C	D	B	E
D	B	E	A	F	C
A	C	F	B	E	D
B	E	D	C	A	F

BRAIN GAME 90

$12 = 2 + 7 + 3$

$15 = 2 + 4 + 9$

$25 = 10 + 6 + 9$

BRAIN GAME 91

a)

21	22	23	24	25
20	17	16	13	12
19	18	15	14	11
6	7	8	9	10
5	4	3	2	1

b)

7	6	5	20	21
8	3	4	19	22
9	2	17	18	23
10	1	16	15	24
11	12	13	14	25

BRAIN GAME 92

1.   c. Pacific

2.   c. Shark

3.   a. Anglerfish

4.   a. Squid

BRAIN GAME 93

f and a

b and h

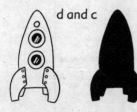
d and c

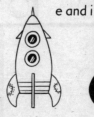 
e and i

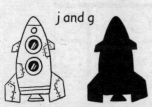
j and g

BRAIN GAME 94

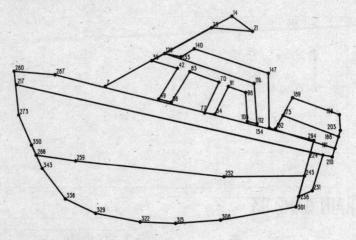

BRAIN GAME 95

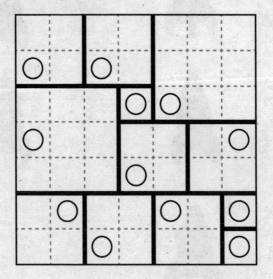

BRAIN GAME 96

a)

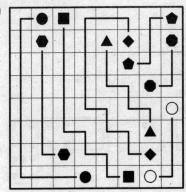

b)

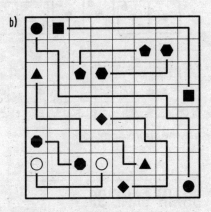

BRAIN GAME 97

24 = 12 + 3 + 9

28 = 10 + 3 + 15

33 = 10 + 14 + 9

BRAIN GAME 98

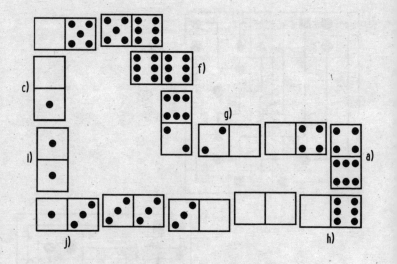

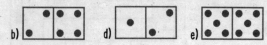

are the spare dominoes

BRAIN GAME 99

22: Burst 7, 19 and 10.

26: Burst 12, 20 and 10.

30: Burst 7, 19 and 12.

BRAIN GAME 100

a and g

d and b

f and c

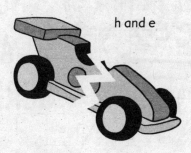

h and e

BRAIN GAME 101

c) d)

are the matching pair

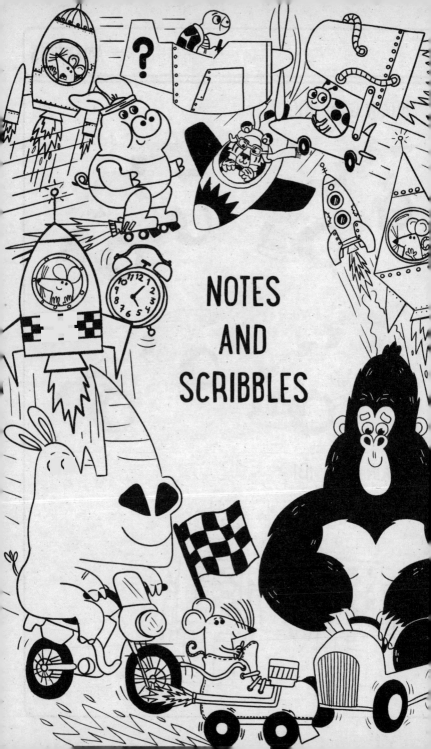

NOTES
AND
SCRIBBLES

NOTES AND SCRIBBLES →

ALSO AVAILABLE:

ISBN 9781780556659

ISBN 9781780556642

ISBN 9781780556192

ISBN 9781780553085

ISBN 9781780552491

ISBN 9781780556185

ISBN 9781780555935

ISBN 9781780555621

ISBN 9781780556635

ISBN 9781780554730

ISBN 9781780555638

ISBN 9781780555409

ISBN 9781780556208

ISBN 9781780553146

ISBN 9781780553078

ISBN 9781780556628

ISBN 9781780554723

ISBN 9781780557106